ARKANSAS RULES OF EVIDENCE

This edition of the Arkansas Rules of Evidence contains the complete text and commentary as revised through May 15, 2020.

ISBN: 9798647213426

Peter Edwards, Esq.
Arkansas Legal Publishing, LLC

Table of Contents

Arkansas Rules of Evidence

Rule 101. Scope.

These rules govern proceedings in the courts of this State to the extent and with the exceptions stated in Rule 1101.

Rule 102. Purpose And Construction.

These rules shall be construed to secure fairness in administration, elimination of unjustifiable expense and delay, and promotion of growth and development of the law of evidence, to the end that the truth may be ascertained and proceedings justly determined.

Rule 103. Rulings On Evidence.

(a) Effect of Erroneous Ruling. Error may not be predicated upon a ruling which admits or excludes evidence unless a substantial right of the party is affected, and

> (1) Objection. In case the ruling is one admitting evidence, a timely objection or motion to strike appears of record, stating the specific ground of objection, if the specific ground was not apparent from the context; or
>
> (2) Offer of proof. In case the ruling is one excluding evidence, the substance of the evidence was made known to the court by offer or was apparent from the context within which questions were asked.

(b) Record of Offer and Ruling. The court may add any other or further statement which shows the character of the evidence, the form in which it was offered, the objection made, and the ruling thereon. It may direct the making of an offer in question and answer form.

(c) Hearing of Jury. In jury cases, proceedings shall be conducted, to the extent practicable, so as to prevent inadmissible evidence from being suggested to the jury by any means, such as making statements or offers of proof or asking questions in the hearing of the jury.

(d) Errors Affecting Substantial Rights. Nothing in this rule precludes taking notice of errors affecting substantial rights although they were not brought to the attention of the court.

Rule 104. Preliminary Questions.

(a) Questions of Admissibility Generally. Preliminary questions concerning the qualification of a person to be a witness, the existence of a privilege, or the admissibility of evidence shall be determined by the court, subject to the provisions of subdivision (b). In making its determination it is not bound by the rules of evidence except those with respect to privileges.

(b) Relevancy Conditioned on Fact. Whenever the relevancy of evidence depends upon the fulfillment of a condition of fact, the court shall admit it upon, or in the court's discretion subject to, the introduction of evidence sufficient to support a finding of the fulfillment of the condition.

(c) Hearing of Jury. Hearings on the admissibility of confessions in criminal cases shall be conducted out of the hearing of the jury. Hearings on other preliminary matters in all cases, shall be so conducted whenever the interests of justice require or, in criminal cases, whenever an accused is a witness, if he so requests.

(d) Testimony by Accused. The accused does not, by testifying upon a preliminary matter, subject himself to cross-examination as to other issues in the case.

(e) Weight and Credibility. This rule does not limit the right of a party to introduce before the jury evidence relevant to weight or credibility.

Rule 105. Limited Admissibility.

Whenever evidence which is admissible as to one [1] party or for one [1] purpose but not admissible as to another party or for another purpose is admitted, the court, upon request, shall restrict the evidence to its proper scope and instruct the jury accordingly.

Rule 106. Remainder Of Or Related Writings Or Recorded Statements.

Whenever a writing or recorded statement or part thereof is introduced by a party, an adverse party may require him at that time to introduce any other part or any other writing or recorded statement which in fairness ought to be considered contemporaneously with it.

Trial court did not abuse its discretion by allowing the state to introduce the transcript of police interviews with the victim, which included parts of the statement that were not introduced by the state, because the defense expressly referred to selective portions of the interviews while attempting to show that the investigator coaxed or cajoled the victim into giving incriminating testimony; thus, the entire transcript of the two interviews were properly admitted to refute a charge of improper influence and to provide context.

Rule 201. Judicial Notice Of Adjudicative Facts.

(a)) Scope of Rule. This rule governs only judicial notice of adjudicative facts.

(b) Kinds of Facts. A judicially noticed fact must be one not subject to reasonable dispute in that it is either (1) generally known within the territorial jurisdiction of the trial court or (2) capable of accurate and ready determination by resort to sources whose accuracy cannot reasonably be questioned.

(c)) When Discretionary. A court may take judicial notice, whether requested or not.

(d) When Mandatory. A court shall take judicial notice if requested by a party and supplied with the necessary information.

(e) Opportunity to be Heard. A party is entitled upon timely request to an opportunity to be heard as to the propriety of taking judicial notice and the tenor of the matter noticed. In the absence of prior notification, the request may be made after judicial notice has been taken.

(f) Time of Taking Notice. Judicial notice may be taken at any stage of the proceeding.

(g) Instructing Jury. The court shall instruct the jury to accept as conclusive any fact judicially noticed.

Rule 301. Presumptions In General In Civil Actions And Proceedings.

(a) Effect. In all actions and proceedings not otherwise provided for by statute or by these rules, a presumption imposes on the party against whom it is directed the burden of proving that the nonexistence of the presumed fact is more probable than its existence.

(b) Inconsistent Presumptions. If presumptions are inconsistent, the presumption applies that is founded upon weightier considerations of policy. If considerations of policy are of equal weight neither presumption applies.

Rule 302. Applicability Of Federal Law In Civil Actions And Proceedings.

In civil actions and proceedings, the effect of a presumption respecting a fact which is an element of a claim or defense as to which federal law supplies the rule of decision is determined in accordance with federal law.

Rule 303. Presumptions In Criminal Cases.

(a) Scope. Except as otherwise provided by statute, in criminal cases, presumptions against an accused, recognized at common law or created by statute, including statutory provisions that certain facts are prima facie evidence of other facts or of guilt, are governed by this rule.

(b) Submission to Jury. The court is not authorized to direct the jury to find a presumed fact against the accused. If a presumed fact establishes guilt or is an element of the offense or negatives a defense, the court may submit the question of guilt or of the existence of the presumed fact to the jury, but only if a reasonable juror on the evidence as a whole, including the evidence of the basic facts, could find guilt or the presumed fact beyond a reasonable doubt. If the presumed fact has a lesser effect, the question of its existence may be submitted to the jury provided the basic facts are supported by substantial evidence or are otherwise established, unless the court determines that a reasonable juror on the evidence as a whole could not find the existence of the presumed fact.

Rule 401. Definition Of "Relevant Evidence".

"Relevant evidence" means evidence having any tendency to make the existence of any fact that is of consequence to the determination of the action more probable or less probable than it would be without the evidence.

Rule 402. Relevant Evidence Generally Admissible - Irrelevant Evidence Inadmissible.

All relevant evidence is admissible, except as otherwise provided by statute or by these rules or by other rules applicable in the courts of this State. Evidence which is not relevant is not admissible.

Rule 403. Exclusion Of Relevant Evidence On Grounds Of Prejudice, Confusion, Or Waste Of Time.

Although relevant, evidence may be excluded if its probative value is substantially outweighed by the danger of unfair prejudice, confusion of the issues, or misleading the jury, or by considerations of undue delay, waste of time, or needless presentation of cumulative evidence.

Rule 404. Character Evidence Not Admissible To Prove Conduct, Exceptions - Other Crimes.

(a) Character Evidence Generally. Evidence of a person's character or a trait of his character is not admissible for the purpose of proving that he acted in conformity therewith on a particular occasion, except:

(1) Character of accused. Evidence of a pertinent trait of his character offered by an accused, or by the prosecution to rebut the same;

(2) Character of victim. Evidence of a pertinent trait of character of the victim of the crime offered by an accused, or by the prosecution to rebut the same, or evidence of a character trait of peacefulness of the victim offered by the prosecution in a homicide case to rebut evidence that the victim was the first aggressor;

(3) Character of witness. Evidence of the character of a witness, as provided in Rules 607, 608, and 609.

(b) Other Crimes, Wrongs, or Acts. Evidence of other crimes, wrongs, or acts is not admissible to prove the character of a person in order to show that he acted in conformity therewith. It may, however, be admissible for other purposes, such as proof of motive, opportunity, intent, preparation, plan, knowledge, identity, or absence of mistake or accident.

Rule 405. Methods Of Proving Character.

(a) Reputation or Opinion. In all cases in which evidence of character or a trait of character of a person is admissible, proof may be made by testimony as to reputation or by testimony in the form of an opinion. On cross-examination, inquiry is allowable into relevant specific instances of conduct.

(b) Specific Instances of Conduct. In cases in which character or a trait of character of a person is an essential element of a charge, claim, or defense, proof may also be made of specific instances of his conduct.

Rule 406. Habit - Routine Practice.

(a) Admissibility. Evidence of the habit of a person or of the routine practice of an organization, whether corroborated or not and regardless of the presence of eyewitnesses, is relevant to prove that the conduct of the person or organization on a particular occasion was in conformity with the habit or routine practice.

(b) Method of Proof. Habit or routine practice may be proved by testimony in the form of an opinion or by specific instances of conduct sufficient in number to warrant a finding that the habit existed or that the practice was routine.

Rule 407. Subsequent Remedial Measures.

Whenever, after an event, measures are taken which, if taken previously, would have made the event less likely to occur, evidence of the subsequent measures is not admissible to prove negligence or culpable conduct in connection with the event. This rule does not require the exclusion of evidence of subsequent measures if offered for another purpose, such as proving ownership, control, or feasibility of precautionary measures, if controverted, or impeachment.

Rule 408. Compromise And Offers To Compromise.

Evidence of (1) furnishing, offering, or promising to furnish, or (2) accepting, offering, or promising to accept, a valuable consideration in compromising or attempting to compromise a claim which was disputed as to either validity or amount, is not admissible to prove liability for, invalidity of, or amount of the claim or any other claim. Evidence of conduct or statements made in compromise negotiations is likewise not admissible. This rule does not require exclusion if the evidence is offered for another purpose, such as proving bias or prejudice of a witness, negativing a contention of undue delay, or proving an effort to obstruct a criminal investigation or prosecution.

Rule 409. Payment Of Medical And Similar Expenses.

Evidence of furnishing, offering or promising to pay medical, hospital, or similar expenses occasioned by an injury is not admissible to prove liability for the injury.

Rule 410. Pleas And Offers.

Evidence of a plea of nolo contendere, whether or not later withdrawn, and of a plea, later withdrawn, of guilty or admission to the charge, or of an offer to plead to the crime charged or any other crime, or of statements made in connection with any of the foregoing pleas or offers, is not admissible in any civil or criminal action, case, or proceeding against the person who made the plea or offer.

HISTORY

Amended November 18, 1996, effective March 1, 1997

Rule 411. Admissibility of evidence of victim's prior sexual conduct.

(a) As used in this rule, unless the context otherwise requires, "sexual conduct" means deviate sexual activity, sexual contact, or sexual intercourse, as those terms are defined by Ark. Code Ann. § 5-14-101.

(b) In any criminal prosecution under Ark. Code Ann. § 5-14-101 et seq. or § 5-26-202, or for criminal attempt to commit, criminal solicitation to commit, or criminal conspiracy to commit an offense defined in any of those sections, opinion evidence, reputation evidence, or evidence of specific instances of the victim's prior sexual conduct with the defendant or any other person, evidence of a victim's prior allegations of sexual conduct with the defendant or any other person, which allegations the victim asserts to be true, or evidence offered by the defendant concerning prior allegations of sexual conduct by the victim with the defendant or any other person if the victim denies making the allegations is not admissible by the defendant, either through direct examination of any defense witness or through cross-examination of the victim or other prosecution witness, to attack the credibility of the victim, to prove consent or any other defense, or for any other purpose.

(c) Notwithstanding the prohibition contained in subsection (b) of this rule, evidence directly pertaining to the act upon which the prosecution is based or evidence of the victim's prior sexual conduct with the defendant or any other person may be admitted at the trial if the relevancy of the evidence is determined in the following manner:

(1) A written motion shall be filed by the defendant with the court at any time prior to the time the defense rests stating that the defendant has an offer of relevant evidence prohibited by subsection (b) of this rule and the purpose for which the evidence is believed relevant.

(2) (A) A hearing on the motion shall be held in camera no later than three (3) days before the trial is scheduled to begin, or at such later time as the court may for good cause permit.

(B) A written record shall be made of the in camera hearing and shall be furnished to the appellate court on appeal.

(C) If, following the in camera hearing, the court determines that the offered proof is relevant to a fact in issue, and that its probative value outweighs its inflammatory or prejudicial nature, the court shall make a written order stating what evidence, if any, may be introduced by the defendant and the nature of the questions to be permitted in accordance with the applicable rules of evidence.

(3) (A) If the court determines that some or all of the offered proof is relevant to a fact in issue, the victim shall be told of the court's order and given the opportunity to consult in private with the prosecuting attorney.

(B) If the prosecuting attorney is satisfied that the order substantially prejudices the prosecution of the case, an interlocutory appeal on behalf of the state may be taken in accordance with Arkansas Rule of Appellate Procedure -Criminal 3.

(d) In the event the defendant has not filed a written motion or a written motion has been filed and the court has determined that the offered proof is not relevant to a fact in issue, any willful attempt by counsel or a defendant to make any reference to the evidence prohibited by subsection (b) of this rule in the presence of the jury may subject counsel or a defendant to appropriate sanctions by the court.

HISTORY

Amended by per curiam order November 15, 2012, effective January 1, 2013.

Rule 501. Privileges Recognized Only As Provided.

Except as otherwise provided by constitution or statute or by these or other rules promulgated by the Supreme Court of this State, no person has a privilege to:

(1) refuse to be a witness;

(2) refuse to disclose any matter;

(3) refuse to produce any object or writing; or

(4) prevent another from being a witness or disclosing any matter or producing any object or writing.

Rule 502. Lawyer-Client Privilege.

(a)) Definitions. As used in this rule:

> (1) A "client" is a person, public officer, or corporation, association, or other organization or entity, either public or private, who is rendered professional legal services by a lawyer, or who consults a lawyer with a view to obtaining professional legal services from him.
>
> (2) A " representative of the client " is one having authority to obtain professional legal services, or to act on advice rendered pursuant thereto, on behalf of the client.
>
> (3) A "lawyer" is a person authorized, or reasonably believed by the client to be authorized, to engage in the practice of law in any state or nation.
>
> (4) A "representative of the lawyer" is one employed by the lawyer to assist the lawyer in the rendition of professional legal services.
>
> (5) A communication is "confidential" if not intended to be disclosed to third persons other than those to whom disclosure is made in furtherance of the rendition of professional legal services to the client or those reasonably necessary for the transmission of the communication.

(b) General Rule of Privilege. A client has a privilege to refuse to disclose and to prevent any other person from disclosing confidential communications made for the purpose of facilitating the rendition of professional legal services to the client (1) between himself or his representative and his lawyer or his lawyer's representative, (2) between his lawyer and the lawyer's representative, (3) by him or his representative or his lawyer or a representative of the lawyer to a lawyer or a representative of a lawyer representing another party in a pending action and concerning a matter of common interest therein, (4) between representatives of the client or between the client and a representative of the client, or (5) among lawyers and their representatives representing the same client.

(c) Who May Claim the Privilege. The privilege may be claimed by the client, his guardian or conservator, the personal representative of a deceased client, or the successor, trustee, or similar representative of a corporation, association, or other organization, whether or not in existence. The person who was the lawyer or the lawyer's representative at the time of the communication is presumed to have authority to claim the privilege but only on behalf of the client.

(d) Exceptions. There is no privilege under this rule: (1) Furtherance of crime of fraud. If the services of the lawyer were sought or obtained to enable or aid anyone to commit or plan to commit what the client knew or reasonably should have known to be a crime or fraud; (2) Claimants through same deceased client. As to a communication relevant to an issue between parties who claim through the same deceased client, regardless of whether the claims are by testate or intestate succession or by inter vivos transaction; (3) Breach of duty by a lawyer or client. As to a communication relevant to an issue of breach of duty by the lawyer to his client or by the client to his lawyer; (4) Document attested by a lawyer. As to a communication relevant to an issue concerning an attested document to which the lawyer is an attesting witness; (5) Joint clients. As to a communication relevant to a matter of common interest between or among two [2] or more clients if the communication was made by any of them to a lawyer retained or consulted in common, when offered in an action between or among any of the clients; or (6) Public officer or agency. As to a communication between a public officer or agency and its lawyers unless the communication concerns a pending investigation, claim, or action and the court determines that disclosure will seriously impair the ability of the public officer or agency to process the claim or conduct a pending investigation, litigation, or proceeding in the public interest.

(e) Inadvertent disclosure. A disclosure of a communication or information covered by the attorney-client privilege or the work-product doctrine does not operate as a waiver if the disclosing party follows the procedure specified in Rule 26(b)(5) of the Arkansas Rules of Civil Procedure and, in the event of a challenge by a receiving party, the circuit court finds in accordance with Rule 26(b)(5)(D) that there was no waiver.

(f) Selective waiver. Disclosure of a communication or information covered by the attorney-client privilege or the work-product doctrine to a governmental office or agency in the exercise of its regulatory, investigative, or enforcement authority does not operate as a waiver of the privilege or protection in favor of non-governmental persons or entities.

COMMENT

Explanatory Note: New subdivision (e) cross-references the 2007 amendment to Rule of Civil Procedure 26(b), which governs inadvertent disclosures of privileged or otherwise protected material during discovery. Under new subdivision (f), disclosure of information covered by the attorney-client privilege or the work-product doctrine to a government agency conducting an investigation of the client does not constitute a general waiver of the information disclosed. In short, this provision adopts a rule of "selective waiver" consistent with the Eighth Circuit's view that disclosure of protected information to the government does not constitute a general waiver, so that the information remains shielded from use by other parties. E.g., Diversified Industries, Inc. v. Meredith, 572 F. 2d 596 (8 th Cir. 1977). This is the minority view among the federal circuits. Most have held that waiver of privileged or protected information to a government agency constitutes a waiver for all purposes. E.g., In re Quest Communications Intern, Inc., 450 F. 3d 1179 (10 th Cir. 2006). Others have recognized selective waiver only if the disclosure was made subject to a confidentiality agreement with the government agency. E.g., Teachers Insurance & Annuity Ass'n v. Shamrock Broadcasting Co., 521 F. Supp 638 (S.D.N.Y. 1981). Subdivision (f) adopts the Eighth Circuit's position, which is also reflected in a draft that the Federal Advisory Committee on Evidence has published for public comment. See http://www.uscourts.gov/rules/Excerpt_EV_Report_Pub.pdf#page=4.

Rule 503. Physician And Psychotherapist-Patient Privilege.

(a)) Definitions. As used in this rule:

(1) A "patient" is a person who consults or is examined or interviewed by a physician or psychotherapist.

(2) A "physician" is a person authorized to practice medicine in any state or nation, or reasonably believed by the patient so to be.

(3) A "psychotherapist" is (i) a person authorized to practice medicine in any state or nation, or reasonably believed by the patient so to be, while engaged in the diagnosis or treatment of a mental or emotional condition, including alcohol or drug addiction, or, (ii) a person licensed or certified as a psychologist under the laws of any state or nation, while similarly engaged.

(4) A communication is "confidential" if not intended to be disclosed to third persons, except persons present to further the interest of the patient in the consultation, examination, or interview, persons reasonably necessary for the transmission of the communication, or persons who are participating in the diagnosis and treatment under the direction of the physician or psychotherapist, including members of the patient's family.

(5) A "medical record" is any writing, document or electronically stored information pertaining to or created as a result of treatment, diagnosis or examination of a patient.

(b) General Rule of Privilege. A patient has a privilege to refuse to disclose and to prevent any other person from disclosing his medical records or confidential communications made for the purpose of diagnosis or treatment of his physical, mental or emotional condition, including alcohol or drug addiction, among himself, physician or psychotherapist, and persons who are participating in the diagnosis or treatment under the direction of the physician or psychotherapist, including members of the patient's family.

(c) Who May Claim the Privilege. The privilege may be claimed by the patient, his guardian or conservator, or the personal representative of a deceased patient. The person who was the physician or psychotherapist at the time of the communication is presumed to have authority to claim the privilege but only on behalf of the patient.

(d) Exceptions:

(1) Proceedings for hospitalization. There is no privilege under this rule for communications relevant to an issue in proceedings to hospitalize the patient for mental illness, if the psychotherapist in the course of diagnosis or treatment has determined that the patient is in need of hospitalization.

(2) Examination by order of court. If the court orders an examination of the physical, mental, or emotional condition of a patient, whether a party or a witness, communications made in the course thereof are not privileged under this rule with respect to the particular purpose for which the examination is ordered unless the court orders otherwise.

(3) Condition and element of claim or defense.

A. There is no privilege under this rule as to medical records or communications relevant to an issue of the physical, mental, or emotional condition of the patient in any proceeding in which he or she relies upon the condition as an element of his or her claim or defense, or, after the patients death, in any proceeding in which any party relies upon the condition as an element of his or her claim or defense.

B. Any informal, ex parte contact or communication with the patient's physician or psychotherapist is prohibited, unless the patient expressly consents. The patient shall not be required, by order of court or otherwise, to authorize any communication with the physician or psychotherapist other than (i) the furnishing of medical records, and (ii) communications in the context of formal discovery procedures.

HISTORY

Amended May 13, 1991, effective July 1, 1991; amended January 22, 1998

Rule 504. Husband-Wife Privilege.

(a) Definition. A communication is confidential if it is made privately by any person to his or her spouse and is not intended for disclosure to any other person.

(b) General Rule of Privilege. An accused in a criminal proceeding has a privilege to prevent his spouse from testifying as to any confidential communication between the accused and the spouse.

(c) Who May Claim the Privilege. The privilege may be claimed by the accused or by the spouse on behalf of the accused. The authority of the spouse to do so is presumed.

(d) Exceptions. There is no privilege under this rule in a proceeding in which one [1] spouse is charged with a crime against the person or property of (1) the other, (2) a child of either, (3) a person residing in the household of either, or (4) a third person committed in the course of committing a crime against any of them.

Rule 505. Religious Privilege.

(a)) Definitions. As used in this rule:

(1) A "clergyman" is a minister, priest, rabbi, accredited Christian Science Practitioner, or other similar functionary of a religious organization, or an individual reasonably believed so to be by the person consulting him.

(2) A communication is "confidential" if made privately and not intended for further disclosure except to other persons present in furtherance of the purpose of the communication.

(b) General Rule of Privilege. A person has a privilege to refuse to disclose and to prevent another from disclosing a confidential communication by the person to a clergyman in his professional character as spiritual adviser.

(c) Who May Claim the Privilege. The privilege may be claimed by the person, by his guardian or conservator, or by his personal representative if he is deceased. The person who was the clergyman at the time of the communication is presumed to have authority to claim the privilege but only on behalf of the communicant.

Rule 506. Political Vote.

(a) General Rule of Privilege. Every person has a privilege to refuse to disclose the tenor of his vote at a political election conducted by secret ballot.

(b) Exceptions. This privilege does not apply if the court finds that the vote was cast illegally or determines that the disclosure should be compelled pursuant to the election laws of the State.

Rule 507. Trade Secrets.

A person has a privilege, which may be claimed by him or his agent or employee, to refuse to disclose and to prevent other persons from disclosing a trade secret owned by him, if the allowance of the privilege will not tend to conceal fraud or otherwise work injustice. If disclosure is directed, the court shall take such protective measures as the interest of the holder of the privilege and of the parties and the interests of justice require.

Rule 508. Secrets Of State And Other Official Information - Governmental Privileges.

(a) If the law of the United States creates a governmental privilege that the courts of this State must recognize under the Constitution of the United States, the privilege may be claimed as provided by the law of the United States.

(b) No other governmental privilege is recognized except as created by the Constitution or statutes of this State.

(c) Effect of sustaining claim. If a claim of governmental privilege is sustained and it appears that a party is thereby deprived of material evidence, the court shall make any further orders the interests of justice require, including striking the testimony of a witness, declaring a mistrial, finding upon an issue as to which the evidence is relevant, or dismissing the action.

Rule 509. Identity Of Informer.

(a) Rule of Privilege. The United States or a state or subdivision thereof has a privilege to refuse to disclose the identity of a person who has furnished information relating to or assisting in an investigation of a possible violation of a law to a law enforcement officer or member of a legislative committee or its staff conducting an investigation.

(b) Who May Claim. The privilege may be claimed by an appropriate representative of the public entity to which the information was furnished.

(c) Exceptions.

> (1) Voluntary disclosure; informer a witness. No privilege exists under this rule if the identity of the informer or his interest in the subject matter of his communication has been disclosed to those who would have cause to resent the communication by a holder of the privilege or by the informer's own action, or if the informer appears as a witness for the government.

(2) Testimony on relevant issue. If it appears in the case that an informer may be able to give testimony relevant to any issue in a criminal case or to a fair determination of a material issue on the merits in a civil case to which a public entity is a party, and the informed public entity invokes the privilege, the court shall give the public entity an opportunity to show in camera facts relevant to determining whether the informer can, in fact, supply that testimony. The showing will ordinarily be in the form of affidavits, but the court may direct that testimony be taken if it finds that the matter cannot be resolved satisfactorily upon affidavit. If the court finds there is a reasonable probability that the informer can give the testimony, and the public entity elects not to disclose his identity, in criminal cases the court on motion of the defendant or on its own motion shall grant appropriate relief, which may include one or more of the following: requiring the prosecuting attorney to comply, granting the defendant additional time or a continuance, relieving the defendant from making disclosures otherwise required of him, prohibiting the prosecuting attorney from introducing specified evidence, and dismissing charges. In civil cases, the court may make any order the interests of justice require. Evidence submitted to the court shall be sealed and preserved to be made available to the appellate court in the event of an appeal, and the contents shall not otherwise be revealed without consent of the informed public entity. All counsel and parties are permitted to be present at every stage of proceedings under this subdivision except a showing in camera at which no counsel or party shall be permitted to be present.

Rule 510. Waiver Of Privilege By Voluntary Disclosure.

A person upon whom these rules confer a privilege against disclosure waives the privilege if he or his predecessor while holder of the privilege voluntarily discloses or consents to disclosure of any significant part of the privileged matter. This rule does not apply if the disclosure itself is privileged.

Rule 511. Privileged Matter Disclosed Under Compulsion Or Without Opportunity To Claim Privilege.

A claim of privilege is not defeated by a disclosure which was (1) compelled erroneously or (2) made without opportunity to claim the privilege.

Rule 512. Comment Upon Or Inference From Claim Of Privilege - Instruction.

(a) Comment or Inference Not Permitted. The claim of a privilege, whether in the present proceeding or upon a prior occasion, is not a proper subject of comment by judge or counsel. No inference may be drawn therefrom.

(b) Claiming Privilege Without Knowledge of Jury. In jury cases, proceedings shall be conducted, to the extent practicable, so as to facilitate the making of claims of privilege without the knowledge of the jury.

(c) Jury Instruction. Upon request, any party against whom the jury might draw an adverse inference from a claim or privilege is entitled to an instruction that no inference may be drawn therefrom.

Rule 601. General Rule Of Competency.

Every person is competent to be a witness except as otherwise provided in these rules.

Rule 602. Lack Of Personal Knowledge.

A witness may not testify to a matter unless evidence is introduced sufficient to support a finding that he has personal knowledge of the matter. Evidence to prove personal knowledge may, but need not, consist of the testimony of the witness himself. This rule is subject to the provisions of Rule 703, relating to opinion testimony by expert witnesses.

Rule 603. Oath Or Affirmation.

Before testifying, every witness shall be required to declare that he will testify truthfully, by oath or affirmation administered in a form calculated to awaken his conscience and impress his mind with his duty to do so.

Rule 604. Interpreters.

An interpreter is subject to the provisions of these rules relating to qualification as an expert and the administration of an oath or affirmation that he will make a true translation.

Rule 605. Competency Of Judge As Witness.

The judge presiding at the trial may not testify in that trial as a witness. No objection need be made in order to preserve the point.

Rule 606. Competency Of Juror As Witness.

(a) At the Trial. A member of the jury may not testify as a witness before that jury in the trial of the case in which he is sitting as a juror. If he is called so to testify, the opposing party shall be afforded an opportunity to object out of the presence of the jury.

(b) Inquiry into Validity of Verdict or Indictment. Upon an inquiry into the validity of a verdict or indictment, a juror may not testify as to any matter or statement occurring during the course of the jury's deliberations or to the effect of anything upon his or any other juror's mind or emotions as influencing him to assent to or dissent from the verdict or indictment or concerning his mental processes in connection therewith, nor may his affidavit or evidence of any statement by him concerning a matter about which he would be precluded from testifying be received, but a juror may testify on the questions whether extraneous prejudicial information was improperly brought to the jury's attention or whether any outside influence was improperly brought to bear upon any juror.

Rule 607. Who May Impeach.

The credibility of a witness may be attacked by any party, including the party calling him.

Rule 608. Evidence Of Character And Conduct Of Witness.

(a) Opinion and Reputation Evidence of Character. The credibility of a witness may be attacked or supported by evidence in the form of opinion or reputation, but subject to these limitations: (1)

the evidence may refer only to character for truthfulness or untruthfulness, and (2) evidence of truthful character is admissible only after the character of the witness for truthfulness has been attacked by opinion or reputation evidence or otherwise.

(b) Specific Instances of Conduct. Specific instances of the conduct of a witness, for the purpose of attacking or supporting his credibility, other than conviction of crime as provided in Rule 609, may not be proved by extrinsic evidence. They may, however, in the discretion of the court, if probative of truthfulness or untruthfulness, be inquired into on cross-examination of the witness (1) concerning his character for truthfulness or untruthfulness, or (2) concerning the character for truthfulness or untruthfulness of another witness as to which character the witness being cross-examined has testified.

The giving of testimony, whether by an accused or by any other witness, does not operate as a waiver of his privilege against self-incrimination when examined with respect to matters which relate only to credibility.

Rule 609. Impeachment By Evidence Of Conviction Of Crime.

(a) General Rule. For the purpose of attacking the credibility of a witness, evidence that he has been convicted of a crime shall be admitted but only if the crime (1) was punishable by death or imprisonment in excess of one [1] year under the law under which he was convicted, and the court determines that the probative value of admitting this evidence outweighs its prejudicial effect to a party or a witness, or (2) involved dishonesty or false statement, regardless of the punishment.

(b) Time Limit. Evidence of a conviction under this rule is not admissible if a period of more than ten [10] years has elapsed since the date of the conviction or of the release of the witness from the confinement imposed for that conviction, whichever is the later date.

(c) Effect of Pardon, Annulment, or Certificate of Rehabilitation. Evidence of a conviction is not admissible under this rule if (1) the conviction has been the subject of a pardon, annulment, certificate of rehabilitation, or other equivalent procedure based on a finding of the rehabilitation of the person convicted, and that person has not been convicted of a subsequent crime which was punishable by death or imprisonment in excess of one [1] year, or (2) the conviction has been the subject of a pardon, annulment, or other equivalent procedure based on a finding of innocence.

(d) Juvenile Adjudications. Evidence of juvenile adjudications is generally not admissible under this rule. Except as otherwise provided by statute, however, the court may in a criminal case allow evidence of a juvenile adjudication of a witness other than the accused if conviction of the offense would be admissible to attack the credibility of an adult and the court is satisfied that admission in evidence is necessary for a fair determination of the issue of guilt or innocence.

(e) Pendency of Appeal. The pendency of an appeal therefrom does not render evidence of a conviction inadmissible. Evidence of the pendency of an appeal is admissible.

Rule 610. Religious Beliefs Or Opinions.

Evidence of the beliefs or opinions of a witness on matters of religion is not admissible for the purpose of showing that by reason of their nature his credibility is impaired or enhanced.

Rule 611. Mode And Order Of Interrogation And Presentation.

(a) Control by Court. The court shall exercise reasonable control over the mode and order of interrogating witnesses and presenting evidence so as to (1) make the interrogation and presentation effective for the ascertainment of the truth, (2) avoid needless consumption of time, and (3) protect witnesses from harassment or undue embarrassment.

(b) Scope of Cross-Examination. Cross-examination should be limited to the subject matter of the direct examination and matters affecting the credibility of the witness. The court may, in the exercise of discretion, permit inquiry into additional matters as if on direct examination.

(c) Leading Questions. Leading questions should not be used on the direct examination of a witness except as may be necessary to develop his testimony. Ordinarily leading questions should be permitted on cross-examination. Whenever a party calls a hostile witness, an adverse party, or a witness identified with an adverse party, interrogation may be by leading questions.

Rule 612. Writing Or Object Used To Refresh Memory.

(a) While Testifying. If, while testifying, a witness uses a writing or object to refresh his memory, an adverse party is entitled to have the writing or object produced at the trial, hearing, or deposition in which the witness is testifying.

(b) Before Testifying. If, before testifying, a witness uses a writing or object to refresh his memory for the purpose of testifying and the court in its discretion determines that the interests of justice so require, an adverse party is entitled to have the writing or object produced, if practicable, at the trial, hearing, or deposition in which the witness is testifying.

(c) Terms and Conditions of Production and Use. A party entitled to have a writing or object produced under this rule is entitled to inspect it, to cross-examine the witness thereon, and to introduce in evidence those portions which relate to the testimony of the witness. If production of the writing or object at the trial, hearing, or deposition is impracticable, the court may order it made available for inspection. If it is claimed that the writing or object contains matters not related to the subject matter of the testimony, the court shall examine the writing or object in camera, excise any portions not so related, and order delivery of the remainder to the party entitled thereto. Any portion withheld over objections shall be preserved and made available to the appellate court in the event of an appeal. If a writing or object is not produced, made available for inspection, or delivered pursuant to order under this rule, the court shall make any order justice requires, but in criminal cases if the prosecution elects not to comply, the order shall be one striking the testimony or, if the court in its discretion determines that the interests of justice so require, declaring a mistrial.

Rule 613. Prior Statements Of Witness.

(a) Examining Witness Concerning Prior Statement. In examining a witness concerning a prior statement made by him, whether written or not, the statement need not be shown nor its contents disclosed to him at that time, but on request the same shall be shown or disclosed to opposing counsel.

(b) Extrinsic Evidence of Prior Inconsistent Statement of Witness. Extrinsic evidence of a prior inconsistent statement by a witness is not admissible unless the witness is afforded an opportunity to explain or deny the same and the opposite party is afforded an opportunity to explain or deny the same and the opposite party is afforded an opportunity to interrogate him thereon, or the interests of justice otherwise require. This provision does not apply to admissions of a party-opponent as defined in Rule 801(d)(2).

Rule 614. Calling And Interrogation Of Witnesses By Court.

(a) Calling by Court. The court, at the suggestion of a party or on its own motion, may call witnesses, and all parties are entitled to cross-examine witnesses thus called.

(b) Interrogation by Court. The court may interrogate witnesses, whether called by itself or by a party.

(c) Objections. Objections to the calling of witnesses by court or to interrogation by it may be made at the time or at the next available opportunity when the jury is not present.

Rule 615. Exclusion Of Witnesses.

At the request of a party the court shall order witnesses excluded so that they cannot hear the testimony of other witnesses, and it may make the order of its own motion. This rule does not authorize exclusion of (1) a party who is a natural person, or (2) an officer or employee of a party that is not a natural person designated as its representative by its attorney, or (3) a person whose presence is shown by a party to be essential to the presentation of his cause.

Rule 616. Right Of Victim To Be Present At Hearing.

Rules text

Notwithstanding any provision to the contrary, in any criminal prosecution, the victim of a crime, and in the event that the victim of a crime is a minor child under eighteen (18) years of age, that minor victim's parents, guardian, custodian or other person with custody of the alleged minor victim shall have the right to be present during any hearing, deposition, or trial of the offense.

Rule 701. Opinion Testimony By Lay Witnesses.

If the witness is not testifying as an expert, his testimony in the form of opinions or inferences is limited to those opinions or inferences which are

(1) Rationally based on the perception of the witness; and

(2) Helpful to a clear understanding of his testimony or the determination of a fact in issue.

Rule 702. Testimony By Experts.

If scientific, technical, or other specialized knowledge will assist the trier of fact to understand the evidence or to determine a fact in issue, a witness qualified as an expert by knowledge, skill, experience, training, or education, may testify thereto in the form of an opinion or otherwise.

Rule 703. Basis Of Opinion Testimony By Experts.

The facts or data in the particular case upon which an expert bases an opinion or inference may be those perceived by or made known to him at or before the hearing. If of a type reasonably relied upon by experts in the particular field in forming opinions or inferences upon the subject, the facts or data need not be admissible in evidence.

Rule 704. Opinion On Ultimate Issue.

Testimony in the form of an opinion or inference otherwise admissible is not objectionable because it embraces an ultimate issue to be decided by the trier of fact.

Rule 705. Disclosure Of Facts Or Data Underlying Expert Opinion.

The expert may testify in terms of opinion or inference and give his reasons therefor without prior disclosure of the underlying facts or data, unless the court requires otherwise. The expert may in any event be required to disclose the underlying facts or data on cross-examination.

Rule 706. Court Appointed Experts.

(a) Appointment. The court, on motion of any party or its own motion, may enter an order to show cause why expert witnesses should not be appointed, and may request the parties to submit nominations. The court may appoint any expert witnesses of its own selection. An expert witness shall not be appointed by the court unless he consents to act. A witness so appointed shall be informed of his duties by the court in writing, a copy of which shall be filed with the clerk, or at a conference in which the parties shall have opportunity to participate. A witness so appointed shall advise the parties of his findings, if any; his deposition may be taken by any party; and he may be called to testify by the court or any party. He shall be subject to cross-examination by each party, including a party calling him as a witness.

(b) Compensation. Expert witnesses so appointed are entitled to reasonable compensation in whatever sum the court may allow. The compensation thus fixed is payable from funds which may be provided by law in criminal cases and civil actions and proceedings involving just compensation for the taking of property. In other civil actions and proceedings the compensation shall be paid by the parties in such proportion and at such time as the court directs, and thereafter charged in like manner as other costs.

(c) Disclosure of Appointment. In the exercise of its discretion, the court may authorize disclosure to the jury of the fact that the court appointed the expert witness.

(d) Parties' Experts of Own Selection. Nothing in this rule limits the parties in calling expert witnesses of their own selection.

Rule 801. Definitions.

The following definitions apply under this Article:

(a) Statement. A "statement" is (1) An oral or written assertion; or (2) Nonverbal conduct of a person, if it is intended by him as an assertion.

(b) Declarant. A "declarant" is a person who makes a statement.

(c) Hearsay. "Hearsay" is a statement, other than one made by the declarant while testifying at the trial or hearing, offered in evidence to prove the truth of the matter asserted.

(d) Statements Which Are Not Hearsay. A statement is not hearsay if:

(1) Prior Statement By Witness. The declarant testifies at the trial or hearing and is subject to cross-examination concerning the statement, and the statement is (i) inconsistent with his testimony and, if offered in a criminal proceeding, was given under oath and subject to the penalty of perjury at a trial, hearing, or other proceeding, or in a deposition, or (ii) consistent with his testimony and is offered to rebut an express or implied charge against him of recent fabrication or improper influence or motive, or (iii) one of identification of a person made after perceiving him; or

(2) Admission By Party-opponent. The statement is offered against a party and is (i) his own statement, in either his individual or a representative capacity, (ii) a statement of which he has manifested his adoption or belief in its truth, (iii) a statement by a person authorized by him to make a statement concerning the subject, (iv) a statement by his agent or servant concerning a matter within the scope of his agency or employment, made during the existence of the relationship, or (v) a statement by a co-conspirator of a party during the course and in furtherance of the conspiracy.

Rule 802. Hearsay Rule.

Hearsay is not admissible except as provided by law or by these rules.

Rule 803. Hearsay Exceptions - Availability Of Declarant Immaterial.

The following are not excluded by the hearsay rule, even though the declarant is available as a witness:

(1) Present Sense Impression. A statement describing or explaining an event or condition made while the declarant was perceiving the event or condition, or immediately thereafter.

(2) Excited Utterance. A statement relating to a startling event or condition made while the declarant was under the stress of excitement caused by the event or condition.

(3) Then Existing Mental, Emotional, or Physical Condition. A statement of the declarant's then existing state of mind, emotion, sensation, or physical condition, such as intent, plan, motive, design, mental feeling, pain, and bodily health, but not including a statement of memory or belief to prove the fact remembered or believed unless it relates to the execution, revocation, identification, or terms of declarant's will.

(4) Statements for Purposes of Medical Diagnosis or Treatment. Statements made for purposes of medical diagnosis or treatment and describing medical history, or past or present symptoms, pain, or sensation, or the inception or general character of the cause or external source thereof insofar as reasonably pertinent to diagnosis or treatment.

(5) Recorded Recollection. A memorandum or record concerning a matter about which a witness once had knowledge but now has insufficient recollection to enable him to testify fully and accurately, shown to have been made or adopted by the witness when the matter was fresh in his memory and to reflect that knowledge correctly. If admitted, the memorandum or record may be read into evidence but may not itself be received as an exhibit unless offered by an adverse party.

(6) Records of Regularly Conducted Business Activity. A memorandum, report, record, or data compilation, in any form, of acts, events, conditions, opinions, or disagnoses [sic], made at or near the time by, or from information transmitted by, a person with knowledge, if kept in the course of a regularly conducted business activity, and if it was the regular practice of that business activity to make the memorandum, report, record, or data compilation, all as shown by the testimony of the custodian or other qualified witness, unless the source of information or the method or circumstances of preparation indicate lack of trustworthiness. The term "business" as used in this paragraph includes business, institution, association, profession, occupation, and calling of every kind, whether or not conducted for profit.

(7) Absence of Entry in Records Kept in Accordance With the Provisions of Paragraph (6). Evidence that a matter is not included in the memoranda, reports, records, or data compilations, in any form, kept in accordance with the provisions of paragraph (6), to prove the nonoccurrence or nonexistence of the matter, if the matter was of a kind of which a memorandum, report, record, or data compilation was regularly made and preserved, unless the sources of information or other circumstances indicate lack of trustworthiness.

(8) Public Records and Reports. To the extent not otherwise provided in this paragraph, records, reports, statements, or data compilations in any form of a public office or agency setting forth its regularly conducted and regularly recorded activities, or matters observed pursuant to duty imposed by law and as to which there was a duty to report, or factual findings resulting from an investigation made pursuant to authority granted by law. The following are not within this exception to the hearsay rule: (i) investigative reports by police and other law enforcement personnel; (ii) investigative reports prepared by or for a government, a public office, or an agency when offered by it in a case in which it is a party; (iii) factual findings offered by the government in criminal cases; (iv) factual findings resulting from special investigation of a particular complaint, case, or incident; and (v) any matter as to which the sources of information or other circumstances indicate lack of trustworthiness.

(9) Records of Vital Statistics. Records or data compilations, in any form, of birth, fetal deaths, deaths, or marriages, if the report thereof was made to a public office pursuant to requirements of law.

(10) Absence of Public Record or Entry. To prove the absence of a record, report, statement, or data compilation, in any form, or the nonoccurrence or nonexistence of a matter of which a record, report, statement, or data compilation, in any form, was regularly made and preserved by a public office or agency, evidence in the form of a

certification in accordance with Rule 902, or testimony, that diligent search failed to disclose the record, report, statement, or data compilation, or entry.

(11) Records of Religious Organizations. Statements of births, marriages, divorces, death, legitimacy, ancestry, relationship by blood or marriage, or other similar facts of personal or family history, contained in a regularly kept record of a religious organization.

(12) Marriage, Baptismal, and Similar Certificates. Statements of fact contained in a certificate that the maker performed a marriage or other ceremony or administered a sacrament, made by a clergyman, public official, or other person authorized by the rules or practices of a religious organization or by law to perform the act certified, and purporting to have been issued at the time of the act or within a reasonable time thereafter.

(13) Family Records. Statements of fact concerning personal or family history contained in family Bibles, genealogies, charts, engravings on rings, inscriptions on family portraits, engravings on urns, crypts, or tombstones, or the like.

(14) Records of Documents Affecting an Interest in Property. The record of a document purporting to establish or affect an interest in property, as proof of the content of the original recorded document and its execution and delivery by each person by whom it purports to have been executed, if the record is a record of a public office and applicable statute authorizes the recording of documents of that kind in that office.

(15) Statements in Documents Affecting an Interest in Property. A statement contained in a document purporting to establish or affect an interest in property if the matter stated was relevant to the purpose of the document, unless dealings with the property since the document was made have been inconsistent with the truth of the statement or the purport of the document.

(16) Statements in Ancient Documents. Statements in a document in existence twenty (20) years or more the authenticity of which is established.

(17) Market Reports, Commercial Publications. Market quotations, tabulations, lists, directories, or other published compilations, generally used and relied upon by the public or by persons in particular occupations.

(18) Learned Treatises. To the extent called to the attention of an expert witness upon cross-examination or relied upon by him in direct examination, statements contained in published treatises, periodicals, or pamphlets on a subject of history, medicine, or other science or art, established as a reliable authority by testimony or admission of the witness or by other expert testimony or by judicial notice. If admitted, the statements may be read into evidence but may not be received as exhibits.

(19) Reputation Concerning Personal or Family History. Reputation among members of his family by blood, adoption, or marriage, or among his associates, or in the community, concerning a person's birth, adoption, marriage, divorce, death, legitimacy, relationship by blood, adoption, or marriage, ancestry, or other similar fact of his personal or family history.

(20) Reputation Concerning Boundaries or General History. Reputation in a community, arising before the controversy, as to boundaries of or customs affecting lands in the community, and reputation as to events of general history important to the community or state or nation in which located.

(21) Reputation as to Character. Reputation of a person's character among his associates or in the community.

(22) Judgment of Previous Conviction. Evidence of a final judgment, (entered after a trial or upon a plea of guilty,) adjudging a person guilty of a crime punishable by death or imprisonment in excess of one (1) year, to prove any fact essential to sustain the judgment, but not including, when offered by the state in a criminal prosecution for purposes other than impeachment, judgments against persons other than the accused. The pendency of an appeal may be shown but does not affect admissibility.

(23) Judgment as to Personal, Family or General History, or Boundaries. Judgments as proof of matters of personal, family or general history, or boundaries, essential to the judgment, if the same would be provable by evidence of reputation.

(24) Other Exceptions. A statement not specifically covered by any of the foregoing exceptions but having equivalent circumstantial guarantees of trustworthiness, if the court determines that (i) the statement is offered as evidence of a material fact; (ii) the statement is more probative on the point for which it is offered than any other evidence which the proponent can procure through reasonable efforts; and (iii) the general purposes of these rules and the interests of justice will best be served by admission of the statement into evidence. However, a statement may not be admitted under this exception unless the proponent of it makes known to the adverse party sufficiently in advance to provide the adverse party with a fair opportunity to prepare to meet it, his intention to offer the statement and the particulars of it, including the name and address of the declarant.

(25) Child Hearsay When Declarant is Available at Trial and Subject to Cross-examination. A statement made by a child under the age of ten (10) years concerning any type of sexual offense, or attempted sexual offense, with, on, or against that child, which is inconsistent with the child's testimony and offered in a criminal proceeding, provided:

> (A) The trial court conducts a hearing outside the presence of the jury and finds that the statement offered possesses a reasonable guarantee of trustworthiness considering the competency of the child both at the time of the out of court statement and at the time of the testimony.
>
> (B) The proponent of the statement gives the adverse party reasonable notice of his intention to offer the statement and the particulars of the statement.
>
> (C) This section shall not be construed to limit the admission of an offered statement under any other hearsay exception or applicable rule of evidence.

HISTORY

Amended May 11, 1992

Rule 804. Hearsay Exceptions - Declarant Unavailable.

(a) Definition of Unavailability. "Unavailability as a witness" includes situations in which the declarant:

(1) Is exempted by ruling of the court on the ground of privilege from testifying concerning the subject matter of his statement;

(2) Persists in refusing to testify concerning the subject matter of his statement despite an order of the court to do so;

(3) Testifies to a lack of memory of the subject matter of his statement;

(4) Is unable to be present or to testify at the hearing because of death or then existing physical or mental illness or infirmity; or

(5) Is absent from the hearing and the proponent of his statement has been unable to procure his attendance (or in the case of a hearsay exception under subdivision (b) (2), (3), or (4), his attendance or testimony) by process or other reasonable means.

A declarant is not unavailable as a witness if his exemption, refusal, claim of lack of memory, inability, or absence is due to the procurement or wrongdoing of the proponent of his statement for the purpose of preventing the witness from attending or testifying.

(b) Hearsay Exceptions. The following are not excluded by the hearsay rule if the declarant is unavailable as a witness:

(1) Former testimony. Testimony given as a witness at another hearing of the same or a different proceeding, or in a deposition taken in compliance with law in the course of the same or another proceeding, if the party against whom the testimony is now offered, or, in a civil action or proceeding a predecessor in interest, had an opportunity and similar motive to develop the testimony by direct, cross, or redirect examination.

(2) Statement under belief of impending death. A statement made by a declarant while believing that his death was imminent, concerning the cause or circumstances of what he believed to be his impending death.

(3) Statement against interest. A statement which was at the time of its making so far contrary to the declarant's pecuniary or proprietary interest, or so far tended to subject him to civil or criminal liability or to render invalid a claim by him against another or to make him an object of hatred, ridicule, or disgrace, that a reasonable man in his position would not have made the statement unless he believed it to be true. A statement tending to expose the declarant to criminal liability and offering to exculpate the accused is not admissible unless corroborating circumstances clearly indicate the trustworthiness of the statement. A statement or confession offered against the accused in a criminal case, made

by a codefendant or other person implicating both himself and the accused, is not within this exception.

(4) Statement of personal or family history.

(i) A statement concerning the declarant's own birth, adoption, marriage, divorce, legitimacy, relationship by blood, adoption, marriage, anecestry [ancestry], or other similar fact of personal or family history, even though declarant had no means of acquiring personal knowledge of the matter stated; or (ii) a statement concerning the foregoing matters and death also, of another person, if the declarant was related to the other by blood, adoption, or marriage or was so intimately associated with the other's family as to be likely to have accurate information concerning the matter declared.

(5) Other exceptions. A statement not specifically covered by any of the foregoing exceptions but having equivalent circumstantial guarantees of trustworthiness, if the court determines that (i) the statement is offered as evidence of a material fact; (ii) the statement is more probative on the point for which it is offered than any other evidence which the proponent can procure through reasonable efforts; and (iii) the general purposes of these rules and the interests of justice will best be served by admission of the statements into evidence. However, a statement may not be admitted under this exception unless the proponent of it makes known to the adverse party sufficiently in advance to provide the adverse party with a fair opportunity to prepare to meet it, his intention to offer the statement and the particulars of it, including the name and address of the declarant.

(6) Child hearsay in civil cases in which the Confrontation Clause of the Sixth Amendment of the Constitution of the United States is not applicable. A statement made by a child under the age of ten (10) years concerning any type of sexual offense, or attempted sexual offense, with, on, or against the child, provided:

(A) The trial court conducts a hearing outside the presence of the jury and finds that the statement offered possesses a reasonable guarantee of trustworthiness. The trial court may employ any factor it deems appropriate including, but not limited to those listed below, in deciding whether the statement is sufficiently trustworthy.

1. The spontaneity of the statement.

2. The lack of time to fabricate.

3. The consistency and repetition of the statement and whether the child has recanted the statement.

4. The mental state of the child.

5. The competency of the child to testify.

6. The child's use of terminology unexpected of a child of similar age.

7. The lack of a motive by the child to fabricate the statement.

8. The lack of bias by the child.

9. Whether it is an embarrassing event the child would not normally relate.

10. The credibility of the person testifying to the statement.

11. Suggestiveness created by leading questions.

12. Whether an adult with custody or control of the child may bear a grudge against the accused offender, and may attempt to coach the child into making false charges.

13. Corroboration of the statement by other evidence.

14. Corroboration of the alleged offense by other evidence.

(B) The proponent of the statement gives the adverse party reasonable notice of his intention to offer the statement and the particulars of the statement.

(C) This section shall not be construed to limit the admission of an offered statement under any other hearsay exception or applicable rule of evidence.

(7) Child hearsay in criminal cases. A statement made by a child under the age of ten (10) years concerning any type of sexual offense against that child, where the Confrontation Clause of the Sixth Amendment of the United States is applicable, provided:

(A) The trial court conducts a hearing outside the presence of the jury, and, with the evidentiary presumption that the statement is unreliable and inadmissible, finds that the statement offered possesses sufficient guarantees of trustworthiness that the truthfulness of the child's statement is so clear from the surrounding circumstances that the test of cross-examination would be of marginal utility. The trial court may employ any factor it deems appropriate including, but not limited to those listed below, in deciding whether the statement is sufficiently trustworthy.

1. The spontaneity of the statement.

2. The lack of time to fabricate.

3. The consistency and repetition of the statement and whether the child has recanted the statement.

4. The mental state of the child.

5. The competency of the child to testify.

6. The child's use of terminology unexpected of a child of similar age.

7. The lack of a motive by the child to fabricate the statement.

8. The lack of bias by the child.

9. Whether it is an embarrassing event the child would not normally relate.

10. The credibility of the person testifying to the statement.

11. Suggestiveness created by leading questions.

12. Whether an adult with custody or control of the child may bear a grudge against the accused offender, and may attempt to coach the child into making false charges.

(B) The proponent of the statement gives the adverse party reasonable notice of his intention to offer the statement and the particulars of the statement.

(C) This section shall not be construed to limit the admission of an offered statement under any other hearsay exception or applicable rule of evidence.

HISTORY

Amended by Per Curiam dated May 11, 1992

Rule 805. Hearsay Within Hearsay.

Hearsay included within hearsay is not excluded under the hearsay rule if each part of the combined statements conforms with an exception to the hearsay rule provided in these rules.

Rule 806. Attacking And Supporting Credibility Of Declarant.

If a hearsay statement, or a statement defined in Rule 801 [d] (2) (iii), (iv), or (v), has been admitted in evidence, the credibility of the declarant may be attacked, and if attacked may be supported, by any evidence which would be admissible for those purposes if declarant had testified as a witness. Evidence of a statement or conduct by the declarant at any time, inconsistent with his hearsay statement, is not subject to any requirement that he may have been afforded an opportunity to deny or explain. If the party against whom a hearsay statement has been admitted calls the declarant as a witness, the party is entitled to examine him on the statement as if under cross-examination.

Rule 901. Requirement Of Authentication Or Identification.

(a) General Provision. The requirement of authentication or identification as a condition precedent to admissiblity [admissibility] is satisfied by evidence sufficient to support a finding that the matter in question is what its proponent claims.

(b) Illustrations. By way of illustration only, and not by way of limitation, the following are examples of authentication or identification conforming with the requirements of this rule:

(1) Testimony of witness with knowledge. Testimony of a witness with knowledge that a matter is what it is claimed to be.

(2) Nonexpert opinion on handwriting. Nonexpert opinion as to the genuineness of handwriting, based upon familiarity not acquired for purposes of the litigation.

(3) Comparison by trier or expert witness. Comparison by the trier of fact or by expert witnesses with specimens which have been authenticated.

(4) Distinctive characteristics and the like. Appearance, contents, substance, internal patterns, or other distinctive characteristics, taken in conjunction with circumstances.

(5) Voice identification. Identification of a voice, whether heard firsthand or through mechanical or electronic transmission or recording, by opinion based upon hearing the voice at any time under circumstances connecting it with the alleged speaker.

(6) Telephone conversations. Telephone conversations, by evidence that a call was made to the number assigned at the time by the telephone company to a particular person or business, if (i) in the case of a person, circumstances, including self-identification, show the person answering to be the one called, or (ii) in the case of a business, the call was made to a place of business and the conversation related to business reasonably transacted over the telephone.

(7) Public records or reports. Evidence that a writing authorized by law to be recorded or filed and in fact recorded or filed in a public office, or a purported public record, report, statement, or data compilation, in any form, is from the public office where items of this nature are kept.

(8) Ancient documents or data compilation. Evidence that a document or data compilation, in any form, (i) is in such condition as to create no suspicion concerning its authenticity, (ii) was in a place where it, if authentic, would likely be, and (iii) has been in existence 20 years or more at the time it is offered.

(9) Process or system. Evidence describing a process or system used to produce a result and showing that the process or system produces an accurate result.

(10) Methods provided by statute or rule. Any method or [of] authentication or identification provided by [the Supreme Court of this State or by] a statute or as provided in the Constitution of this State.

Rule 902. Self-Authentication.

Extrinsic evidence of authenticity as a condition precedent to admissibility is not required with respect to the following:

(1) Domestic Public Documents Under Seal. A document bearing a seal purporting to be that of the United States, or of any state, district, commonwealth, territory, or insular possession thereof, or the Paname [Panama] Canal Zone, or the Trust Territory of the Pacific Islands, or of a political subdivision, department, officer, or agency thereof, and a signature purporting to be an attestation or execution.

(2) Domestic Public Documents Not Under Seal. A document purporting to bear the signature in his official capacity of an officer or employee of any entity included in

paragraph (1), having no seal, if a public officer having a seal and having official duties in the district or political subdivision of the officer or employee certifies under seal or that the signer has the official capacity and that the signature is genuine.

(3) Foreign Public Documents. A document purporting to be executed or attested in his official capacity by a person authorized by the laws of a foreign country to make the execution or attestation, and accompanied by a final certification as to the genuineness of the signature and official position (i) of the executing or attesting person, or (ii) of any foreign official whose certificate of genuineness of signature and official position relates to the execution or attestation or is in a chain of certificate of genuineness of signature and official position relating to the execution or attestation. A final certification may be made by a secretary of embassy or legation, consul general, consul, vice consul, or consular agent of the United States or a diplomatic or consular official of the foreign country assigned or accredited to the United States. If reasonable opportunity has been given to all parties to investigate the authenticity and accuracy of official documents, the court may for good cause shown order that they be treated as presumptively authentic without final certification or permit them to be evidenced by an attested summary with or without final certification.

(4) Certified Copies of Public Records. A copy of an official record or report or entry therein, or of a document authorized by law to be recorded or filed and actually recorded or filed in a public office, including data compilations in any form, certified as correct by the custodian or other person authorized to make the certification, by certificate complying with paragraph (1), (2), or (3), or complying with any law of the United States or of this State.

(5) Official Publications. Books, pamphlets, or other publications issued by public authority.

(6) Newspapers and Periodicals. Printed material purporting to be newspapers or periodicals.

(7) Trade Inscriptions and the Like. Inscriptions, signs, tags, or labels purporting to have been affixed in the course of business and indicating ownership, control, or origin.

(8) Acknowledged Documents. Documents accompanied by a certificate of acknowledgement executed in the manner provided by law by a notary public or other officer authorized by law to take acknowledgements.

(9) Commercial Paper and Related Documents. Commercial paper, signatures thereon, and documents relating thereto to the extent provided by general commercial law.

(10) Presumptions Created by Law. Any signature, document, or other matter declared by any law of the United States or of this State, to be presumptively or prima facie genuine or authentic.

Rule 903. Subscribing Witness' Testimony Unnecessary.

The testimony of a subscribing witness is not necessary to authenticate a writing unless required by the laws of the jurisdiction whose laws govern the validity of the writing.

Rule 1001. Definitions.

For purposes of this Article the following definitions are applicable:

(1) Writings and Recordings. "Writings" and "recordings" consist of letters, words, sounds, or numbers, or their equivalent, set down by handwriting, typewriting, printing, photostating, photographing, magnetic impulse, mechanical or electronic recording, or other form of data compilation.

(2) Photographs. "Photographs" include still photographs, x-ray films, video tapes, and motion pictures.

(3) Original. An "original" of a writing or recording is the writing or recording itself or any counterpart intended to have the same effect by a person executing or issuing it. An "original" of a photograph includes the negative or any print therefrom. If data are stored in a computer or similar device, any printout or other output readable by sight, shown to reflect the data accurately, is an "original."

(4) Duplicate. A "duplicate" is a counterpart produced by the same impression as the original, or from the same matrix, or by means of photography, including enlargements and miniatures, or by mechanical or electronic re-recording, or by chemical reproduction, or by other equivalent techniques which accurately reproduce the original.

Rule 1002. Requirement Of Original.

To prove the content of a writing, recording, or photograph, the original writing, recording, or photograph is required, except as otherwise provided in these rules or by [rules adopted by the Supreme Court of this state or by] statute.

Rule 1003. Admissibility Of Duplicates.

A duplicate is admissible to the same extent as an original unless (1) a genuine question is raised as to the authenticity or continuing effectiveness of the original or (2) in the circumstances it would be unfair to admit the duplicate in lieu of the original.

Rule 1004. Admissibility Of Other Evidence Of Contents.

The original is not required, and other evidence of the contents of a writing, recording, or photograph is admissible if:

(1) Originals Lost or Destroyed. All originals are lost or have been destroyed, unless the proponent lost or destroyed them in bad faith;

(2) Original Not Obtainable. No original can be obtained by any available judicial process or procedure;

(3) Original in Possession of Opponent. At a time when an original was under the control of the party against whom offered, he was put on notice, by the pleadings or otherwise, that the contents would be a subject of proof at the hearing; and he does not produce the original at the hearing; or

(4) Collateral Matters. The writing, recording or photograph is not closely related to a controlling issue.

Rule 1005. Public Records.

The contents of an official record, or of a document authorized to be recorded or filed and actually recorded or filed, including data compilations in any form, if otherwise admissible, may be proved by copy, certified as correct in accordance with Rule 902 or testified to be correct by a witness who has compared it with the original. If a copy complying with the foregoing cannot be obtained by the exercise of reasonable diligence, other evidence of the contents may be admitted.

Rule 1006. Summaries.

The contents of voluminous writings, recordings, or photographs which cannot conveniently be examined in court may be presented in the form of a chart, summary, or calculation. The originals, or duplicates, shall be made available for examination or copying, or both, by other parties at a reasonable time and place. The court may order that they be produced in court.

Rule 1007. Testimony Or Written Admission Of Party.

Contents of writings, recordings, or photographs may be proved by the testimony or deposition of the party against whom offered or by his written admission, without accounting for the nonproduction of the original.

Rule 1008. Functions Of Court And Jury.

Whenever the admissibility of other evidence of contents of writings, recordings, or photographs under these rules depends upon the fulfillment of a condition of fact, the question whether the condition has been fulfilled is ordinarily for the court to determine in accordance with the provisions of Rule 104. However, when an issue is raised whether (1) the asserted writing ever existed, or (2) another writing, recording, or photograph produced at the trial is the original, or (3) other evidence of contents correctly reflects the contents, the issue is for the trier of fact to determine as in the case of other issues of fact.

Rule 1009. Translation Of Foreign-Language Documents And Recordings.

(a) Translations. A translation of foreign-language documents and recordings, including transcriptions, that is otherwise admissible under the Arkansas Rules of Evidence shall be admissible upon the affidavit of a "qualified translator," as defined in paragraph (h) of this rule, setting forth the qualifications of the translator, and certifying that the translation is fair, accurate, and complete. This affidavit, along with the translation and the underlying foreign language documents or recordings, shall be served upon all parties at least forty-five (45) days before the date of trial.

(b) Objections. Any party may object to the accuracy of another party's translation by pointing out the specific inaccuracies of the translation and by stating with specificity what the objecting party contends is a fair and accurate translation. This objection shall be served upon all parties at least fifteen (15) days before the date of trial.

(c) Effect of Failure to Object or Offer Conflicting Translation. If no conflicting translation or objection is timely served, the court shall admit a translation submitted under paragraph (a) without need of proof, provided however that the underlying foreign-language documents or recordings are otherwise admissible under the Arkansas Rules of Evidence. Failure to serve a conflicting translation under paragraph (a), or failure to timely and properly object to the accuracy of a translation under paragraph (b), shall preclude a party from attacking or offering evidence contradicting the accuracy of the translation at trial.

(d) Effect of Objections or Conflicting Translations. In the event of conflicting translations under paragraph (a), or if objections to another party's translation are served under paragraph (b), the court shall determine whether there is a genuine issue as to the accuracy of a material part of the translation to be resolved by the trier of fact.

(e) Expert Testimony of Translator. Except as provided in paragraph (c), this rule does not preclude the admission of a translation of foreign-language documents and recordings at trial either by live testimony or by deposition testimony of a qualified translator.

(f) Varying of Time Limits. The court, upon motion of any party and for good cause shown, may enlarge or shorten the time limits set forth in this rule.

(g) Court Appointment. The court, if necessary, may appoint a qualified translator, the reasonable value of whose services shall be taxed as court costs.

(h) Qualified Translator. A "qualified translator" is an interpreter satisfying the requirements established by the Arkansas Supreme Court in In Re: Certification for Foreign Language Interpreters in Arkansas Courts, 338 Ark. App'x. 827 (1999) and Administrative Order Number 11. A Registry of Interpreters is maintained by the Administrative Office of the Courts.

Rule 1101. Rules Applicable.

(a) Except as otherwise provided in subdivision (b), these rules apply to all actions and proceedings in the [courts of this State].

(b) Rules Inapplicable. The rules other than those with respect to privileges do not apply in the following situations:

(1) Preliminary questions of fact. The determination of questions of fact preliminary to admissibility of evidence when the issue is to be determined by the court under Rule 104 (a).

(2) Grand jury. Proceedings before grand juries.

(3) Miscellaneous proceedings. Proceedings for extradition or rendition; [preliminary examination] detention hearing in criminal cases; sentencing, or granting or revoking

probation; issuance of warrants for arrest, criminal summonses, and search warrants; and proceedings with respect to release on bail or otherwise.

(4) Contempt proceedings in which the court may act summarily.

Rule 1102. Title.

These rules shall be known as the Arkansas Rules of Evidence and may be cited as A.R.E. Rule-.

HISTORY

Acts 1975 (Extended Sess., 1976), No. 1143, 1, p. 2799; adopted October 13, 1986

Made in the USA
Monee, IL
04 December 2020